How to Find Freedom and Wealth Through Spending:

Financial independent while living in wealth

By

how to find freedom and wealth through spending

STEWART MCDANIEL

Copyright © STEWART MCDANIEL 2022. All rights reserved

Before this document is duplicated or reproduced in any manner, the publisher's consent must be gained.

Therefore, the contents within can neither be stored electronically, transferred, nor kept in a database. Neither in part nor in full can the document be copied, scanned, faxed, or retained without approval from the publisher or creator.

how to find freedom and wealth through spending

Table of content

Introduction   3

Chapter 1
Pay off your debts and resist the allure of buy-now-pay-later deals   7

Chapter 2
Design an Investment Strategy that will Maximize Your Financial Potential   23

Chapter 3
Create a Financial Independence Plan   42

Chapter 4
Decide on Real Estate Investment   46

Chapter 5
By maximizing your work and starting a side business, you can reach financial independence sooner   50

Chapter 6
Obtain a degree, but don't overlook the importance of love 56

Chapter 7
The most important things to take away from all this book 63

how to find freedom and wealth through spending

Introduction

Why should I care? Choosing wisely will assist you in achieving financial independence.

Reading this book suggests that you are interested in the concept of financial freedom. Everyone is, right? However, you must first comprehend why you want this objective before you can begin to work toward it. What precisely do you hope to accomplish? What does having financial freedom mean to you personally?

Maybe you're looking for it for your health or happiness.
Financial independence might entail having no worries about money or job-related stress.

how to find freedom and wealth through spending

Or perhaps you want to have peace of mind knowing that you can cover family expenses and a hospital bill if you or a loved one becomes unwell.

Maybe your anxiety about job security is similar to that of many others. Are you concerned that your supervisor dislikes you? Are you worried that a coworker would (figuratively) stab you in the back because you work in a competitive field? Does your position suggest that you might lose your job if the company merges? Perhaps, in general, finding a job with security doesn't seem to be as simple as it once was. You would have the freedom to work only when you wanted to, rather than because you had to. Or perhaps you are concerned about a potential recession as you observe the current situation of the world and the economy.

how to find freedom and wealth through spending

Well, having financial independence would enable you to weather that storm.

Of course, there are a lot of other factors why you could want financial freedom.

For instance, you could wish to impress your parents. Or perhaps you'd want to spend more time with your kids or avoid working for an organization that goes against your moral standards.

In your quest for financial freedom, there are several factors you should take into account, which this book covers. It provides answers to queries such as, How should I divide up my funds among different financial assets?

What should my real estate investment budget be? How about my vehicle? Also, maybe unexpectedly, how does love factor into the situation?

how to find freedom and wealth through spending

Let's get going!

This book will teach you how to pay off your debts in what sequence; how the 30/30/3 rule for real estate purchases operates; and why it's important to prioritize love and knowledge.

Chapter 1
Pay off your debts and resist the allure of buy-now-pay-later deals

Take time to consider your monthly money and how you spend it. How much money can you save each month? What are you doing to maximize your earnings to achieve this financial independence? What exactly is financial independence?

What You Should Understand About Financial Independence

Definition of financial independence
Many people define financial freedom on their own terms. You can consider yourself set if you've paid off all of your outstanding

bills, or you might not consider yourself financially independent until you win the lotto.

"I think of it as having the confidence that you can always pay your expenses and also having money left over so you can go out at a restaurant if you want or save up for a vacation," I try to stick to the 50/30/20 rule of budgeting. That means you can devote 50% of your after-tax income to your necessities, such as housing and food. You'll set aside 30% of your money for wants like entertainment and apparel. The remaining 20% should be allocated to debts, savings goals (such as a rainy day fund or emergency fund), and other financial objectives.

Money, as the cliché goes, does not buy happiness. But that doesn't stop the majority of people from wishing for financial freedom. Having a good grasp on your money—where it comes from and where it goes—is regarded as a sign of maturity and success (and many people see financial independence as part of adulthood).

Financial independence can also be defined as having a net worth that is 20 times your

how to find freedom and wealth through spending

average gross income or having enough investments to produce enough passive income to pay your costs. You should ideally have both.

How quickly you achieve financial independence is determined by how much

work you are willing to put in, how much you save and invest, and how much risk you are willing to take. Consider your savings again: if you can save 50% of your after-tax money, that's the equivalent of one year's living costs. Seventy percent covers two years of living expenditures. And what if that isn't a possibility right now? Save 20% of your income and you'll have one year's worth of living expenses in four years. The sensible decision is to save and live frugally in your early years to reap the benefits later.

how to find freedom and wealth through spending

If you want to achieve financial freedom, you must earn, save, invest, and plan. But, before we get into how to invest, we must first address a sensitive subject: debt.

Many of us end ourselves in debt because we strive to live lives we can't afford. Buy-now, pay-later deals abound, tempting us to skip the hard work and go directly for the rewards. Giving in to them, on the other hand, is a sure way to never achieve financial freedom.

Of course, debt is sometimes unavoidable: a natural disaster, unanticipated medical expenses, or, as a single parent, your finances are just stretched too thin. But, if you're serious about achieving financial independence, paying off debt should be your top priority.

Taking care of your debts

Credit card

Credit card debt occurs when a credit card company's customer purchases an item or service through the card system.

When a consumer fails to repay the corporation, the debt escalates due to the accrual of interest and penalties.

The average APR is around 15%, but some are as high as 29.99%. So pay off your credit cards right away and just use them for rewards and insurance. Never carry a balance forward since you will be taken advantage of

how to find freedom and wealth through spending

by credit card issuers.

To confront the credit card debt front on, it is helpful to first devise and stick to a plan.

Prioritize paying off high-interest cards or cards with the smallest amounts.

You will pay less interest altogether if you pay more than the monthly minimum.

If you carry credit card amounts from month to month, paying it off quickly may be easier than you think. The trick is to make a decent plan and stick to it.

These four tactics might assist you in determining which path to adopt to swiftly pay off any credit card debt.

Concentrate on one debt at a time

how to find freedom and wealth through spending

Do you have a credit card balance on more than one? If this is the case, make sure you always pay the minimum on each card.

Then, pay down the complete sum on one card at a time.

More than the bare minimum
Examine your credit card bill. It takes much longer to pay off your credit card bill if you only pay the minimum balance. You will pay less interest overall if you pay more than the minimum. Your credit card company is required to show this on your statement so you can see how it affects your bill.

Debt consolidation
Debt consolidation allows you to combine several higher-interest balances into one with a lower rate, allowing you to pay off your debt faster without increasing your payment amounts. Here are two common methods for

debt consolidation: Balance transfers and Making use of your home equity.

Examine your spending

Begin by categorizing your monthly expenses, such as groceries, transportation, housing, and entertainment. Your credit card statement can be a valuable resource because many issuers categorize your expenditures. Look for spots where you can make cuts. Then use the money you've saved to pay off your debts.

Debt for a car

Even though your auto loan interest rate is modest, the value of your car depreciates every month.
But first, let's go over the auto loan process so you know what's going on behind the scenes.

When you finance an automobile, you are borrowing money from a lender to "purchase" it. The vehicle loan is the amount you borrow and the arrangement to repay that money over time. And your automobile payment is the monthly loan payment.

An automobile loan is divided into three parts:

The principal : is the loan's total amount. **Interest:** is the amount of money added to your automobile payment each month by your bank or lender in exchange for lending you money.
Term: The length of time you have to repay the loan.

Sounds simple enough, doesn't it? However, auto salespeople are adept at brushing the tiny print under the rug to make it appear as if you're receiving a terrific deal.

The truth is that financing a car costs you more in the long term than buying it outright.

How to Get Out of a Car Loan

Let's speak about how to get out of that auto loan now that you know what a total waste of car payments is. You basically have two choices: pay off the debt or sell the car. Which should you choose? That depends on how you answer two questions:

1. Can you pay off your debts and keep your car for two years?

If so, repay the loan. Otherwise, sell it.

how to find freedom and wealth through spending

2. Does the total value of all your vehicles (items with motors) exceed half of your annual income?

If so, you should sell it. Otherwise, pay off the loan.

That's the easy answer, but let's look at how each choice works.

Repay the loan.
If you can pay off your auto loan in two years and the entire worth of your vehicles is less than half your salary, it's time to get serious about it. How serious is it? Serious enough to create a budget, drastically reduce your expenditures, and perhaps even start a side

hustle. Do everything you can to put as much money as possible toward your car loan.

But we have one more question for you: Do you truly adore your car? Like, do you love it enough to allow it to keep you in debt for a longer period?

Even if you can pay it off in less than two years, you may want to sell it and buy something cheaper for the time being. That way, you can make much more progress toward debt freedom.

Remember, the sooner you get out of debt, the sooner you can start accumulating true wealth!

Sell the vehicle.

how to find freedom and wealth through spending

If your car payments are sapping your income and preventing you from becoming debt-free in two years, it's time to let them go (aka sell your car). We understand that this is upsetting, and we're not saying you can't drive that car again. But you deserve to be able to own your car rather than having it own you.

The first step is to determine the current value of your vehicle.

Because the used car market is hot right now, you might be able to get even more for it. Start spreading the word about what you're selling next.

Try market places, social media, word of mouth, and so on. Then, when you sell it, you'll have enough money to pay off the loan and buy something in your price range without spending much.

Follow the "one-tenth rule of car purchasing." That is, don't spend more than one-tenth of your annual gross income on a car.

Driving about in your five-year-old, more-mileage-than-I-care-to-mention hatchback won't kill you until you can afford to buy your shiny, new automobile entirely!

Loan for students

Student debt refers to college tuition loans that are due after the student graduates or leaves school.

If you haven't attended college yet and want to get a degree, look for an affordable school.

As a result, you will be able to pay off or clear your loan within four years of graduating.

Mortgage

A mortgage is a sort of loan that is used to buy or keep a home, land, or other types of real estate. The borrower agrees to repay the lender over time, usually in the form of a series of regular payments divided into principal and interest. The property is then used as security for the loan.

Consider your mortgage. This is a complicated topic that we will discuss in real estate investment.

Chapter 2
Design an Investment Strategy that will Maximize Your Financial Potential

An investment strategy is a method of thinking that impacts how you select the investments in your portfolio. The greatest techniques should help you reach your financial goals and develop your wealth while keeping a level of risk that helps you sleep at night. The method you adopt may influence everything from what types of assets you have to how you approach buying and selling those assets.

If you're ready to start investing, a decent rule of thumb is to ask yourself some fundamental questions: What are your goals? How much time until you retire? How comfortable are you with risk? Do you know how much you wish to invest in stocks, bonds, or an alternative?

This is when investment methods come into play.
The best investment methods enhance the money investors make and limit their exposure to risk.

The plan will vary based on your end investing goal and its timing, your risk tolerance, and how engaged you want to be in choosing particular investments.

Many investors combine numerous tactics to obtain the most customized plan to meet their scenario.

Beginner investment strategies

If you're not yet investing, there are some basic steps you may take to begin. If you have a 401(k) via your job, be sure you're enrolled and investing at least enough of your salary to obtain any company match; then choose investments that are aligned with your goals. You should note that most 401(k)s have relatively few investment alternatives, thus the options for strategy inside those vehicles are usually limited.

Another approach to invest for retirement is to open an IRA through a brokerage account, which will provide you access to a wider range of investments than your 401(k) may offer. You can also trade using a brokerage account for long-term goals other than retirement.

Popular investing techniques

There are different ways to approach investing, but here are some of the more popular investing ideas to explore.

Buy-and-hold investing

It's always helpful when things have a clear label, and you can't get much clearer than "buy and hold."

Buy-and-hold strategists seek stocks they feel will perform well over many years. The objective is to not become rattled when the

market dips or decreases in the near term but to stick to your investments and stay the course.

Buy-and-hold works only if investors believe in their investment's long-term potential through those short-term falls. This technique encourages investors to carefully assess their assets whether they are broad index funds or a rising young stock for their long-term growth prospects upfront. But once this initial labor is done, holding investments saves time you would have spent trading, and often outperforms the profits of more-active trading tactics.

Active investing

Active investors like trading more frequently and opportunistically to capitalize on market swings.

Stock traders may utilize technical analysis, the study of past market data such as trading volume or price movements, to assist anticipate where market prices might go.

Active trading encompasses multiple tactics based on pricing, such as swing or spread trading, and can also incorporate momentum and event-driven strategies. Momentum investing aims to discover and follow trends currently in favor to profit off of market mood. Event-driven investing techniques try to capture pricing disparities during corporate transitions and events, such as during mergers and acquisitions, or a distressed company filing for bankruptcy.

Dollar-cost averaging

The toughest hurdle to timing the markets is getting it correctly on a consistent basis.

For those investors leery of trying their luck on market timing but still wanting a favorable entry point into the market, the method of dollar-cost averaging may appeal.

Investors that dollar-cost average their way into the market spread their stock or fund purchases out across time, buying the same amount at regular periods. Doing so helps to "smooth" out the purchase price over time as you purchase more shares when the stock price is down and buy fewer shares when the stock price is high. Over time, you obtain a better average entry price and lessen the impact of market volatility on your portfolio.

Index investing

While there are active and passive techniques to investing, there are also active and passive investments themselves when picking

between various types of funds. Investors typically utilize mutual funds, index funds, and exchange-traded funds (ETFs) to build their investment portfolio since funds allow access to a selection of securities, generally equities and bonds, through one vehicle. Funds allow investors to benefit from diversification, spreading the investment risk over numerous securities to help balance

how to find freedom and wealth through spending

volatility.

Active funds employ a portfolio or fund manager to handpick particular investments to populate the fund based on proprietary research, analysis, and forecasts. The manager's goal is to outperform the fund's matching index or benchmark. Passive funds, such as index funds and most ETFs, merely imitate an underlying index, giving the

investor a similar performance to that particular index.

Some mutual funds have high expense ratios or high minimum investments (or both). But investors may often escape the highest of such expenses by comparison shopping across mutual funds, or by selecting index funds and ETFs, which tend to provide lower expense ratios than actively managed funds. Given the reduced cost of passive funds and the tough task of beating the benchmark facing portfolio managers, index or passive investing frequently produces greater total returns over time.

Growth investing

Growth investing entails buying shares of developing firms that are positioned to grow at an above-average pace in the future.

Companies like this generally offer a unique product or service that competitors can't readily copy. While growth stocks are far from a sure thing, their attractiveness is that they might expand in value considerably quicker than established equities if the underlying business takes off.

Growth investors are willing to pay a premium price for these businesses in exchange for their robust future growth potential.

New technologies generally fall within this group. For example, if someone believes that home purchasers are going to transfer more from banks to online mortgage lenders with a faster application procedure, they can invest in the lender they anticipate will become dominant in that market.

Investors might also look toward expanding geographies or companies to find growth. As they industrialize, emerging markets or developing economies normally are more volatile but also grow at a faster pace relative to their more-developed rivals.

Companies are valued by market capitalization, or market cap, which is calculated by their total outstanding shares available times the market price of the shares.

Small-cap stocks, and shares of firms usually valued at $2 billion in market cap or less, providing investors with greater potential risk but also greater possible return due to their faster growth trajectory.

Value Investing

Value investing is the bargain shopping of investment methods. By purchasing what they think to be inexpensive stocks with great long-term prospects, value investors attempt to reap the advantages when the companies attain their true potential in the years ahead. Value investing usually demands a relatively active hand, someone who is prepared to study the market and news for signals on which stocks are inexpensive at any given time.

Think about it like this: A value investor might grab up shares of a historically successful automobile business when its stock price dips following the release of a horrible new model, so long as the investor feels the new model was a fluke and that the company would bounce back over time.

Value investing is considered a contrarian technique since investors are going against the grain or investing in stocks or industries currently out of favor.

A subset of investors takes value investing a step further by not just investing in cheaper stocks and sectors but intentionally hunting out the cheapest ones out there to invest in so-called deep value.

Income investing

Investment strategies can help investors achieve a particular aim; for instance, producing a steady income stream.

Many investors use income investing to help fund their living expenditures, particularly while transitioning into retirement.

There are many investments that can create income, from dividend-paying stocks to bonds and CD ladders to real estate.

Socially responsible investing

Social issues such as climate change and racial justice influence life on a day-to-day level. Socially responsible investing (SRI) aims to create positive change in society while also generating positive returns.

In addition to investment performance, SRI investors look into a company's business practices and revenue sources to ensure they're aligned with their personal values.

Some investors apply SRI by excluding stocks of companies that go against their moral compass; for instance, they would exclude investments in "sin" equities or tobacco- and alcohol-related industries. Others consciously put their investing resources toward subjects they care about, such as sustainable energy companies.

Principles of investment strategies
Whatever investment strategy you choose, it's important to consider your investing goals.

Where your investment style will fit in the following categories depends on numerous factors:

Everything from your age to your income and even your comfort level doing it yourself will help determine what your portfolio will look like.

Long-term goals vs. short-term

When investing for long-term goals those five years or more in the future it may make sense to use higher-yielding (but more volatile) instruments like equities and stock ETFs. But there are wise methods to pursue short-term financial objectives, too. If you're saving for a down payment on a house, you may want to store those savings in a more stable environment, like CDs or a high-yield savings account.

Since you have a shorter time period for your money to grow with a goal like this, there is less time to weather the volatility of the stock market.

Long-term financial goals, such as retirement, can handle the vagaries of the market. Since such assets will be in the

market for longer — provided the investor can stay the course when there are substantial changes in the short term — there is less need to worry about those shorter-term drops.

These long-term investments are better served by a mix of stocks and bonds or stock mutual funds.

Low-risk vs. high-risk investing strategy
Investment strategies always come with some amount of risk, and in almost every way risk and reward are linked.

Investors who pursue higher rewards are usually taking bigger risks.

For example, a bank CD is insured by the Federal Deposit Insurance Corp. and has virtually no risk. It also pays very little in return.

A young tech startup's stock, on the other hand, is likely higher-risk, but there is a chance it could explode in value.

There are many shades of risk in between, but whatever path you choose, make sure you're prepared to deal with them.

Do-it-yourself vs. hiring professional help

Investors have many choices when it comes to managing their investment portfolio. How involved do you want to be in the investing process? How much do you already know about investing?

Beginner investors may prefer to hand their savings off to a Robo-advisor, an automated, low-cost investing service, rather than take on the challenge of making all the choices themselves.

More advanced investors might opt to take a more active role, whether that means trading every day or just keeping tabs on their portfolios. Active investing can be a lot of work and may not give you higher returns than passive investing strategies.

Chapter 3
Create a Financial Independence Plan

Financial independence requires a strategy, just like most other aspects of life. To increase your wealth, it's crucial to think carefully about where and when to invest your savings.

Saving more money will help you become financially independent faster. Additionally, you should maximize your tax-advantaged retirement account contributions while simultaneously maximizing your taxable account growth.

Depending on your situation and stage of life, you should invest your money in stocks, bonds, and real estate.

You should also invest a modest portion of your resources as an "emergency fund" in risk-free assets.

Later, if you want to diversify, think about investing in alternative assets including collectibles, art, wine, farming, and cryptocurrencies.

Depending on your personality and age, I provide you with the three allocation models to think about.

First model

Conventional, this model, is a low-risk choice. Invest in equities, bonds, properties, and other safe investments. For individuals who don't mind working over their state's retirement age, this is fantastic.

Second model

Risk-taking by New Life is more aggressive. This is for those who, at the age of about 40, want to restart their lives. Think about making some alternative investments, such as private equity, venture capital, or cryptocurrencies.

Third model

By making an investment in yourself and starting your own business, you can achieve financial independence sooner in life.

In your twenties, start developing some passive income streams. And start a side business that will bring in enough money to cover your basic living costs.

Whichever model you select, you'll probably have amassed more wealth by the time you're 50 than the average individual. But keep in mind that your financial gains are not assured. The secret is to diversify so that you can weather economic upswings and downturns. Here are some fundamental guidelines: After the age of 40, avoid having more than 50% of your net worth in a single asset class.

Then, once your wealth has grown, transition to capital preservation.

Chapter 4
Decide on Real Estate Investment

First and foremost, it's crucial to keep in mind that you're pursuing financial freedom here, so your best option might not be the nicest — the town apartment in the city might be the better option right now rather than the cottage in the countryside.

Only use renting as a temporary housing solution, please. While you're determining where to live and starting your profession, it enables you to keep your options open. However, you should buy one once you've decided that you'll stay in one spot for at least five years.

how to find freedom and wealth through spending

And if you're ready, how much can you spend on your primary residence?

Owning real estate in addition to your home residence is a terrific way to increase your wealth, but you must follow the 30/30/3 rule when making the purchase to avoid going overboard.

First, the monthly mortgage payment should not exceed 30 percent of your gross income. This is especially crucial if you have a little salary since if you spend more, you won't have as much left over for other expenses.

Secondly, make sure you have 30% of the home's value in liquid or somewhat liquid assets. That is divided into two-thirds for a down payment.

Your financial reserve in case of unforeseen circumstances makes up the remaining third.

Don't give in to the urge to put down less than 20% of the purchase price. In a recession, those homeowners who don't have a buffer and do this suffer the most.

Thirdly, don't spend more on your home than three times your gross annual revenue. Therefore, if your income is $100,000, don't spend more than $30,000 on a buy. Your monthly payment will remain within your means as a result.

Whether it's equity or monthly income flow from a multi-unit, the real estate boasts one of the highest returns on investment.

You may buy a multi-family property with as little as 3.5 percent down. The simplest approach to begin your investment portfolio is in this manner. After a brief period of habitation, buy your next one.

During a recession, real estate typically does better than equities and bonds, and it gains from increased rents and property values during a strong economy. For instance, the COVID-19 pandemic had the following effects: markets crashed in March 2020, yet real estate values remained stable.

Then, when things looked better, there was a surge in demand for real estate.

Chapter 5
By maximizing your work and starting a side business, you can reach financial independence sooner.

Your work helps you invest when you're young, which in turn helps you earn more money and eventually achieve financial independence.

The ideal job is one that pays well and you enjoy doing it. Make sure you're at least well-paid for your work if you can't locate a position you enjoy.

You can always fit in your favorite activities on your own schedule.

how to find freedom and wealth through spending

Build the strongest foundation you can over the first 21 years of your career.

When you're in your forties, this will then give you more possibilities.

Find a job in a wealthy area if you're just starting out in your career, and put in the effort to become skilled at something. Find a course while you're still in college that will qualify you to work in a high-paying field; ideally, it should pay six figures right out of college or within five years of joining. Venture capital, investment banking, strategic consulting, IT, engineering, real estate, and oil are examples of industries that accomplish this. Don't forget to take a look at the future pension plans that employers offer, particularly those in the public sector.

But the competition for lucrative positions is fierce.

There is probably only a 1% chance that you will be invited for an interview. You may have a 25% probability of getting the job following the interview. Apply repeatedly until you land the position you want.

It's time to start your side business if you are stuck in a low-paying position or are unable to quit or change jobs.

"Work while others are sleeping so you can eventually play while others are working" this approach is for people pursuing financial freedom to adopt.

Your job is probably going to be your main source of income, so you should make the most of it by getting promoted and getting paid more.

But if you want to hasten your path to financial independence, you also need a side business.

You can have a large or little side business. Get up a little earlier to work on it before you leave for work if you prefer the mornings. If not, work on it later in the day. You can increase your productivity by over 700 hours a year by working two hours a day. Even though it's never too late to start, it's best to start your side hustle when you're young since as you age, your energy may start to diminish.

However, what can you really do?

Getting a second job that you can do outside of your regular working hours, whether it's a contract or freelance job, will allow you to participate in the "gig economy."

It might involve working a physically demanding shift or perhaps it's something done online, like creating logos for start-ups, writing for hire, or doing voice-over work.

However, in each of those cases, you are still doing the hiring. Find a long-term side business where you can create your own brand, which is preferable. For instance, you may provide a series of piano lessons under your own brand name rather than teaching piano privately or in groups online.

After that, you won't need to put in any additional effort to sell your course to others.

Your side business might even turn into your primary business over time. When you are certain of two things—that you genuinely enjoy what you are doing and that you are earning enough to meet your basic needs—is the appropriate moment to do it.

Chapter 6
Obtain a degree, but don't overlook the importance of love

Education more than anything else frees you. It supports your decision-making regarding your career, investments, and life partner. Additionally, it boosts your confidence and aids in business development. In the end, it makes you happier.

There are many free courses available online, so it need not be formal education. Even those who disagree with you have something to teach you.
The most important thing is to stay open and to always learn. There is always new information to learn!

Remember that attending a prestigious university is not as important as you might

how to find freedom and wealth through spending

think if you're thinking about getting a degree.

Yes, it might offer your parents something to talk about, and hiring employers might be more impressive when you're just out of college. But after a few years of professional experience, no one is concerned because they can base their decision on your track record.

The bottom line is that you should enroll in the best school you can afford, but avoid accruing six figures in student debt in an effort to increase your chances of landing a job after graduation.

Now let's talk about love
The big question is: Would you rather be impoverished and in love or affluent and

alone? You're not actually required to respond to it! Neither circumstance is ideal. Money is much better spent on your partner and, eventually, perhaps your children.

The fact is that we require both love and money equally. Without it, we might experience financial hardship. And if we were to have children, we would worry about our ability to provide for their future.

Sadly, it's also true that financial difficulties play a role in 36% of divorces.

The good news is that you can have both love and wealth.

Make finding a life companion your first goal if you're single. If you already have one, take care of it every single day!

Also keep in mind that if you truly care about someone, you'll want to support them in achieving financial independence.

Your next thought after falling in love might be: Should we get married? From a purely financial perspective, tax and social security are the two factors to take into account.

Cohabitation may be preferable for high earners who have a combined income of $500,000 because they may be subject to an income tax penalty. However, regulations can change at any time, so consult your tax advisor.

Also keep in mind that being married may provide more financial advantages when it comes to collecting social security, particularly in the event that one partner passes away.

how to find freedom and wealth through spending

That spouse's social security payments would thereafter continue to be paid to the surviving spouse.

Keep your wedding expenses to a minimum if you do decide to get married! Spending shouldn't exceed 10% of your total income, 3% of your combined pre-tax retirement savings, 50% of your combined side hustle gross income, or 10% of your annual passive investment income, in that order.

Spend as much as your parents want to spend as a final option.

Why would you refuse their generosity, after all?

The ideal arrangement for bank accounts is to have both joint and separate accounts. Having a separate account provides you with

how to find freedom and wealth through spending

some financial freedom to spend how you choose.

It also serves as insurance in case something happens that causes your spouse's and your combined assets to become subject to probate.

And what about children? When you are both financially and emotionally stable is when you should get pregnant if you desire children.

But in any case, you need to have your finances in order; otherwise, you'll be stressed out and constantly worried.

Help your children financially when they reach adulthood. Charge interest instead, and give them a deadline to pay you back.

You can choose to forgive the loan only once they are prepared to pay it back, not before. Let them take pride in the fact that they, too, were successful on their own.

Chapter 7
The most important things to take away from all this book

Start by figuring out why you want to be financially independent; this will help you focus your efforts.

Second, start paying off your debts, starting with your credit cards.

Third, keep in mind the guidelines for buying a car (spend no more than 10% of your annual salary on it) and the 30/30/3 rule for buying a house (save 30% of the purchase price for the down payment and buffer, and don't spend more than 3 times your gross annual income on it).

Fourth, make room for love since, without someone to share it with, what good is money?

Here is some additional sound counsel. Follow the 70/30 rule while making decisions.

The most challenging aspect of making difficult decisions is committing in a way that prevents self-doubt. That necessitates two steps:

You must act on your choice; moreover

You must be prepared to be proven wrong.

Frequently, we lack the knowledge necessary to draw valid conclusions. However, if we think in terms of probability rather than binary absolutes, we not only develop a stronger attitude for making judgments, but we also increase the likelihood that those decisions will be successful.

The 70/30 philosophy is what, then?
It implies that between 70% and 30% of the complete knowledge is required to make a decision.

how to find freedom and wealth through spending

You should take a risk if you can predict that a choice has at least a 70% chance of working out. At the same time, it's a recognition that 30% of the time, your choice will be less than ideal and you'll have to live with the consequences.

With less than 30%, you'll probably make a bad selection, and with more than 70%, you'll take too long and someone else will make the choice for you!

The key message here is to strive to make wise decisions more than bad ones. However, people cannot avoid making decisions altogether out of fear of making mistakes.

The right amount of speed and precision is required.

The fact is that you'll never have all the data you require to make the ideal choice.

You must rely on your experience and instincts for the remaining matters.

If you adopt this mindset, you'll undoubtedly experience some regrets along the way, but you'll also grow from them. Additionally, your choices will probably be more successful in the long run.

I wish you well as you work toward financial freedom!

www.ingramcontent.com/pod-product-compliance
Lightning Source LLC
Chambersburg PA
CBHW070318220526
45465CB00004B/1899